CARDBOARD

Eco
Activities

Written by
Louise Nelson

CRABTREE
PUBLISHING COMPANY
WWW.CRABTREEBOOKS.COM

CRABTREE
PUBLISHING COMPANY
WWW.CRABTREEBOOKS.COM

Author: Louise Nelson

Editorial Director: Kathy Middleton

Editors: Robin Twiddy, Ellen Rodger

Proofreader: Crystal Sikkens

Cover/Interior Design: Jasmine Pointer

**Production coordinator and
Prepress technician:** Margaret Amy Salter

Print coordinator: Katherine Berti

Photo Credits

All images are courtesy of Shutterstock.com, unless otherwise specified. With thanks to Getty Images, Thinkstock Photo and iStockphoto.
Paper Texture Throughout – Borja Andreu. Front Cover – New Africa, Olga1818, Macrovector, Dragon Images, KaliAntye. 4–5 – Africa Studio, VGstockstudio. 6–7 – Philip Kinsey, Whyoem, nelik, Dmitri_st, Aquarius Studiov. 8–9 – galitsin, vipman, Nadiia Korol. 10–11 – Vannaweb, Sergei Kolesnikov. 12–13 – Kolpakova Daria, Orapin Thepsuttinun, Svhl, 123object, lord_photon, sirsir. 14–15 – Mountain Brothers, Dmitry Ishimov, springsky, Kolpakova Daria, Pattern image, cmgirl, Studio KIWI, kozirsky. 16–17 – Huguette Roe, Teresa Kasprzycka. 18–19 – Katerina Morozova, Krakenimages.com. 20–21 – KaliAntye, Olya Detry. 22–23 – New Africa, Africa Studio, Yuganov Konstantin, Luis Louro, wavebreakmedia, Gines Romero.

Library and Achives Canada Cataloguing in Publication

Title: Cardboard : eco activities / written by Louise Nelson.
Names: Nelson, Louise, 1981- author.
Description: Includes index.
Identifiers: Canadiana (print) 20200356852 | Canadiana (ebook) 20200356860
  ISBN 9781427128591 (hardcover) |
  ISBN 9781427128638 (softcover) |
  ISBN 9781427128676 (HTML)
Subjects: LCSH: Cardboard art—Juvenile literature. | LCSH: Paperboard—
  Recycling—Juvenile literature. | LCSH: Refuse as art material—Juvenile
  literature. | LCSH: Handicraft—Juvenile literature.
Classification: LCC TT870 .N45 2021 | DDC j745.54—dc23

Library of Congress Cataloging-in-Publication Data

Names: Nelson, Louise, author.
Title: Cardboard eco activities / Louise Nelson.
Description: New York, NY : Crabtree Publishing Company, 2021. |
  Series: Eco activities | Includes index.
Identifiers: LCCN 2020045625 (print) | LCCN 2020045626 (ebook) |
  ISBN 9781427128591 (hardcover) |
  ISBN 9781427128638 (paperback) |
  ISBN 9781427128676 (ebook)
Subjects: LCSH: Waste paper--Recycling--Juvenile literature. | Paper industry-
  -Environmental aspects--Juvenile literature. | Recycling industry--Juvenile
  literature. | Refuse and refuse disposal--Juvenile literature.
Classification: LCC TS1120.5 .N45 2021 (print) | LCC TS1120.5 (ebook) |
  DDC 676/.288--dc23
LC record available at https://lccn.loc.gov/2020045625
LC ebook record available at https://lccn.loc.gov/2020045626

Crabtree Publishing Company

www.crabtreebooks.com   1-800-387-7650
Published by Crabtree Publishing Company in 2021

Printed in the U.S.A./122020/CG20201014

**Published in Canada
Crabtree Publishing**
616 Welland Avenue
St. Catharines, Ontario
L2M 5V6

**Published in the United States
Crabtree Publishing**
347 Fifth Ave
Suite 1402-145
New York, NY 10016

CONTENTS

Words that are **bolded** can be found in the glossary on page 24.

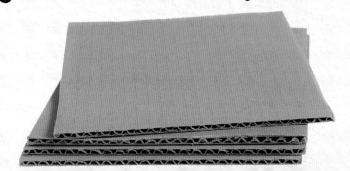

A CARDBOARD CRISIS

WAIT! Don't throw that cardboard in the garbage! Cardboard can be **recycled,** but there is so much more you can do with it first!

Did you know?
A lot of things we throw away can be used again and again!

Cardboard is made from trees. In order to make new cardboard, more trees have to be cut down. So, what should we do to avoid losing our forests?

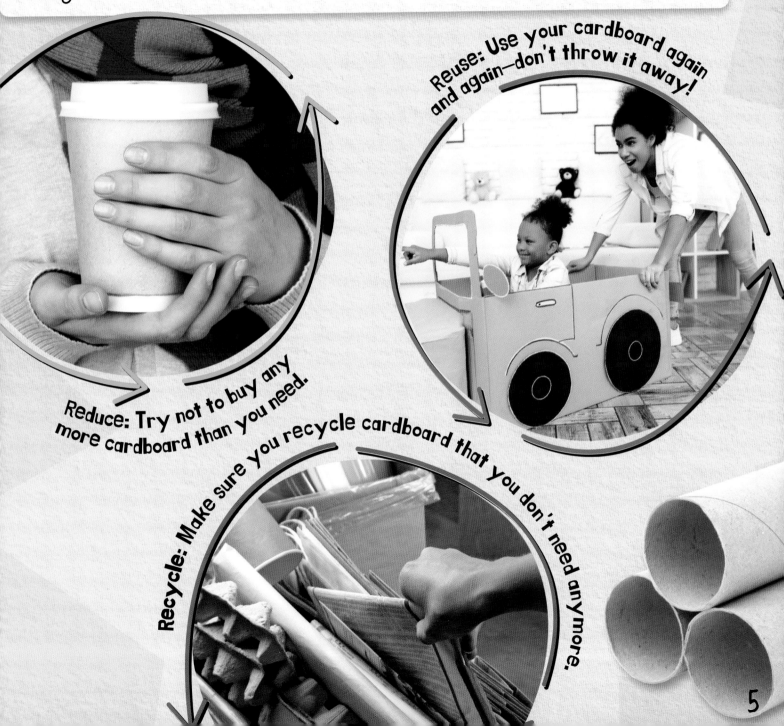

Reuse: Use your cardboard again and again—don't throw it away!

Reduce: Try not to buy any more cardboard than you need.

Recycle: Make sure you recycle cardboard that you don't need anymore.

WHAT IS CARDBOARD?

Cardboard is a material. We use materials, such as wood, glass, fabric, and metal, to make things. Materials have properties. Properties tell us what the material is like.

The Properties of Cardboard

Can be made into a lot of shapes and colors

Opaque (not see-through)

Not very hard—
you can scratch,
cut, and fold it

Absorbs water

Made by people from
a natural material

Can be thin or thick

CARDBOARD CITY

Your toys and dolls can enjoy an **eco-friendly** life in a cardboard dollhouse!

Don't paint your boxes. Use markers instead. They look good and are eco-friendly, so you can recycle everything afterward!

You will need:

- Cardboard boxes
- Masking tape
- Scissors
- Markers
- Glue
- Fabric scraps (maybe reuse some old clothes!)
- Your favorite dolls and toys

! Safety first! Always ask an adult for help with scissors.

STEP 1. Get your cardboard box.

STEP 2. Ask an adult to help you cut windows and a roof.

STEP 3. Stick your boxes together with the masking tape.

STEP 4. Use the markers to draw bricks, windowsills, and other details.

You could even stack smaller boxes together to make different floors!

STEP 5. Use any leftover cardboard to make furniture for your house. You can make tiny chairs and tables, and cut little curtains from fabric.

Did you know?
Recycled paper and cardboard are often used to make toilet paper rolls, newspaper, and egg cartons!

CARDBOARD CHAMELEON

This colorful chameleon will brighten up your bedroom wall!

This makes a great class project. Could you cover a whole wall with rainbow chameleons?

You will need:

- Thick corrugated cardboard (this can be found in boxes)
- Paints in a lot of colors
- Paintbrushes
- Glue
- Pasta shapes, pom-poms, sequins, and crafting decorations
- Scissors

Clean as You Go

Don't forget to put newspaper down in your working area and wear an apron.

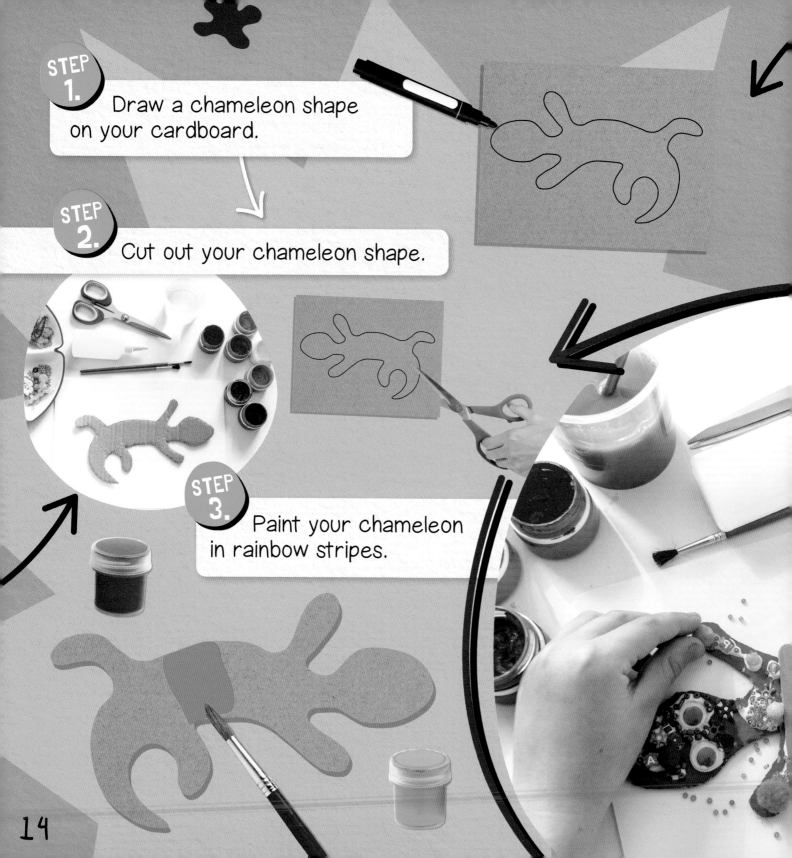

STEP 1.
Draw a chameleon shape on your cardboard.

STEP 2.
Cut out your chameleon shape.

STEP 3.
Paint your chameleon in rainbow stripes.

14

STEP 4. Glue colored decorations on to match your stripes.

Try painting pasta shapes to match your stripes.

STEP 5. Glue on some googly eyes and you're done!

Don't forget—
you can't recycle cardboard that has been painted. Make sure you only paint what you need, then recycle the rest.

15

CAREFUL WITH CARDBOARD!

Cardboard that isn't reused or recycled can end up in **landfills**.
Cardboard in landfills **rots** away and releases a **gas** called methane.
Methane can be bad for the **environment**.

Every year, paper and cardboard that took around 1 billion trees to make is thrown away in the U.S.

But it's OK! There are some easy ways to help. Recycle all of your cardboard waste so it doesn't go to landfills. If you make sure to put it in the correct recycling bin, you can make a big difference!

ON A (TOILET) ROLL

The cardboard tube inside a toilet paper roll can have all kinds of uses. We think this activity is the most fun!

One tree produces about 200 rolls of toilet paper.

You will need:

- Tubes from toilet paper rolls
- Paint and paintbrushes
- Paper
- Googly eyes
- Decorations

19

Toilet paper tubes can be made into all kinds of characters. Use the paper and paint to decorate your tubes and create a whole range of characters! What will you create?

Spring animals?

Scary monsters?

Squashed flat to make a fish?

Try making characters from one of your favorite books.

Toilet paper tubes can be used to make all kinds of things. The only limit is your imagination! You could make a whole set of animals and have your own zoo!

21

CARDBOARD COSTUMES

Cardboard is so useful as a material that it can become almost anything… and so can you!

A knight in cardboard armor!

Roar! A cardboard dinosaur!

A fresh fruit stand!

To infinity...

Go exploring!

Sail the seven seas!

I want to be a rock star!

GLOSSARY

absorbs	Takes in or soaks up
eco-friendly	Does not harm nature
environment	The natural world
gas	A thing that is like air, which spreads out to fill any space available
landfill	Where waste is buried
natural material	Something that comes from nature
opaque	Can't be seen through
recycle	Use again to make something else
rots	When something natural breaks down

INDEX